PETER RABBIT
and His Friends
WORD BOOK

CHATHAM RIVER PRESS
New York

Created and manufactured by arrangement with Ottenheimer Publishers, Inc.
Copyright © 1988 Ottenheimer Publishers, Inc.
This 1988 edition published by Ottenheimer Publishers, Inc.,
for Chatham River Press, a division of Arlington House, Inc.,
distributed by Crown Publishers, Inc., 225 Park Avenue South,
New York, New York 10003
All rights reserved
Printed in the United States of America
h g f e d c b a

FURNITURE

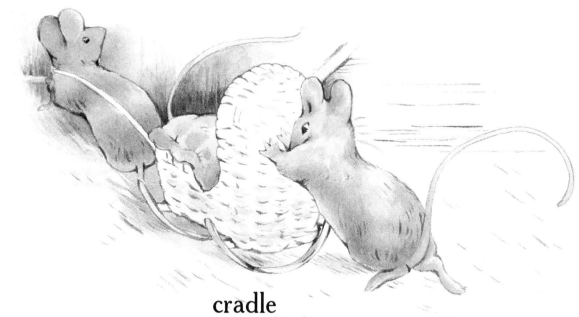

cradle

chair

mirror

rocking chair

table

grandfather
clock

bed

AT HOME

pans

herbs

fire

glasses

kitchen

turnips

picture

pillow

wall

blanket

bedroom

bed

bowls

floor

basket

CLOTHES

apron

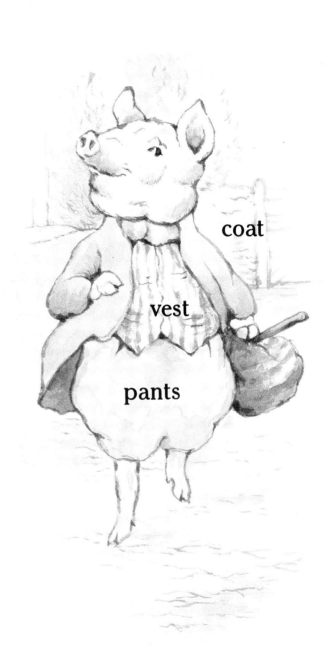

coat

vest

pants

dress

bonnet

jacket

shawl

shoe

curtains

hat

window seat

clock

dresser

shirt

washbowl

towel

brush

comb

FOOD

strawberry

onions

oranges

pears

ham

fish

pie

lettuce

blackberries

peas

carrots

platters

door

shelf

dishes

cabinet

pitcher

kettle

teapot

cup

spoon

FOREST FRIENDS

owl

hedgehog

squirrels

fox

mole

mice

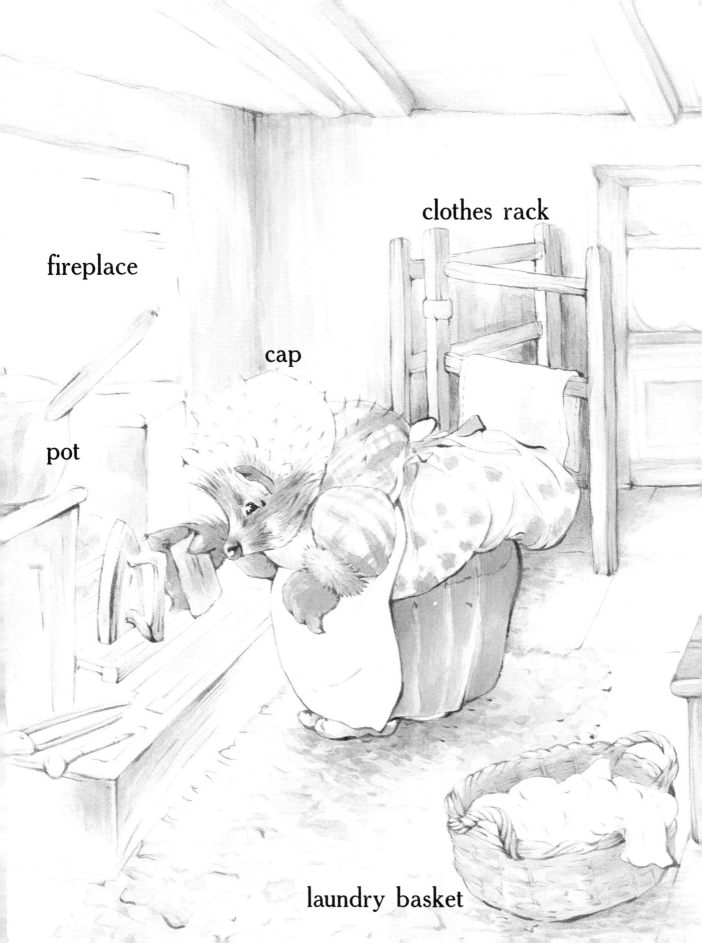

fireplace

clothes rack

cap

pot

laundry basket

clothesline

clothespins

iron

washtub

LAUNDRY ROOM

POND FRIENDS

tortoise

newt

stickleback

frog

trout

water beetle

butterfly

trees

leaves

rocks

twigs

lake

island

raft

anchor

THE LAKE

boat

oar

grass

WEATHER

snow

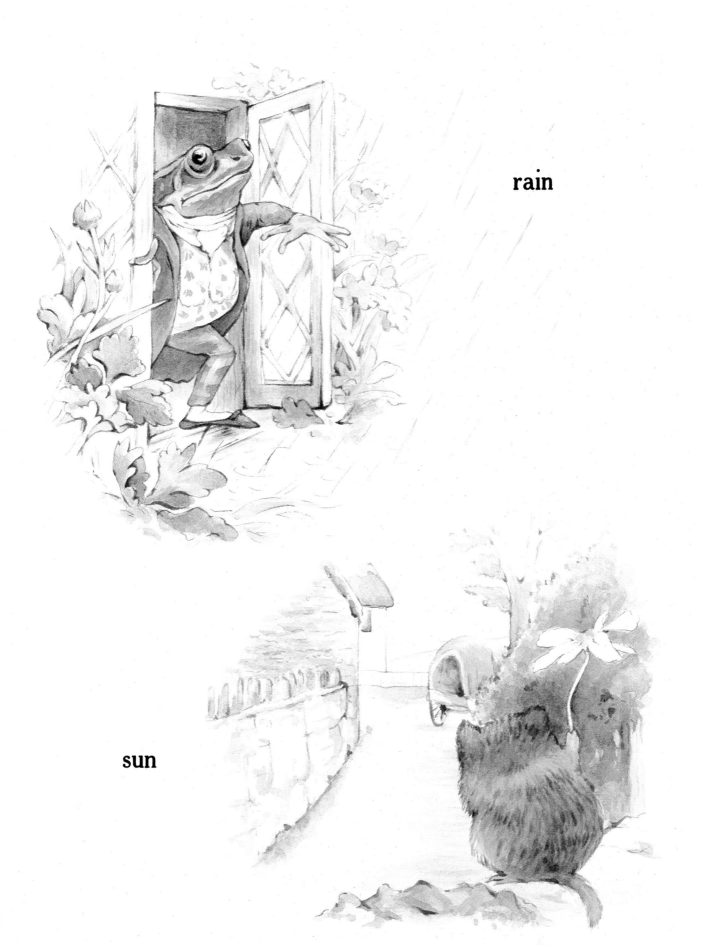

rain

sun

reeds

cattails

water lily

lily pad

pond

minnows

FISHING

TOOLS

watering can

bucket

shovel

spade

rake

wheelbarrow

scarecrow

gate

cabbage

path

soil

birds

beans

GARDEN

TOOL SHED

broom

flowerpots

flowers

bushes

goldfish

FARM
FRIENDS

rabbit

dog

puppies

duck

ducklings

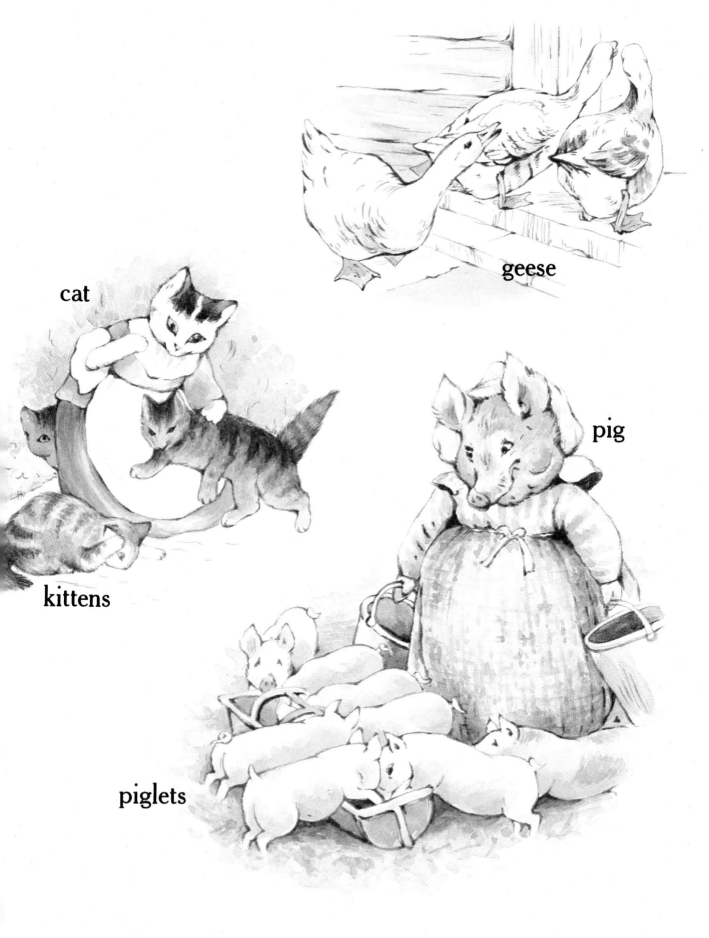

geese

cat

kittens

pig

piglets

stall

FARMYARD

rooster

chicken

hay

SEASONS

spring

summer

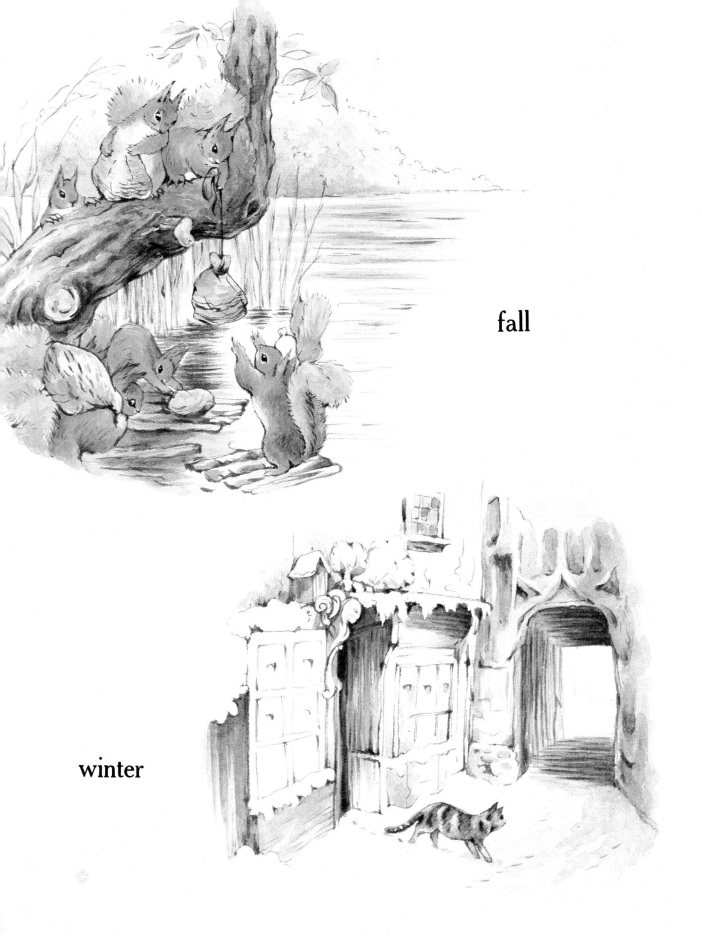

fall

winter

groceries

bottles

scale

string

package

counter

customers

FLOWERS

geranium

buttercups

daisies

foxgloves

pansies

SEWING ROOM

candle

ribbon

cloth